Teen.

D0590298

AMAZING MATHS JOBS

COLIN HYNSON

First published in Great Britain
in 2016 by Wayland

Editor: Victoria Brooker
Produced by Tall Tree Ltd
Editor: Jon Richards
Designer: Darren Jordan

ISBN: 978 1 5263 0010 2
10 9 8 7 6 5 4 3 2 1

Wayland
An imprint of Hachette
Children's Group
Part of Hodder and Stoughton
Carmelite House
50 Victoria Embankment
London EC4Y 0DZ

An Hachette UK Company
www.hachette.co.uk
www.hachettechildrens.co.uk

Printed and bound in China

The website addresses (URLs) included in this
book were valid at the time of going to press.
However, it is possible that contents or addresses
may have changed since the publication of this
book. No responsibility for any such changes can
be accepted by either the author or the Publisher.

CONTENTS

MATHS

Jobs in maths	**4**
Cracking codes	**6**
Transport planner	**8**
Mapping the planet	**10**
Feeding the world	**12**
The bigger picture	**14**
Sports statistics	**16**
Shaping our climate	**18**
Visual effects	**20**
Digital forensics	**22**
Dealing with disaster	**24**
Further and faster	**26**
The next big thing	**28**
Glossary	**30**
Index	**32**

JOBS IN MATHS

A QUALIFICATION IN MATHS CAN TAKE YOU FROM HI-TECH MOTOR RACING TO THE EXCITING REALM OF MOVIE MAKING!

Welcome to the world of working in mathematics. Studying maths is really worthwhile, because it opens doors to a whole range of interesting, exciting and unusual jobs — amazing jobs in mathematics.

Studying maths doesn't mean you'll be stuck in a lecture theatre or a classroom. There are jobs in code breaking, food production and disaster relief, to name a few. Find out what each job is all about, as well as the rewards of doing the job.

▶ Formula One designers use high-end maths skills to work out how air will flow over their cars.

STEM STANDS FOR SCIENCE, TECHNOLOGY, ENGINEERING AND MATHS. AS SCIENCE, TECHNOLOGY, AND ENGINEERING INDUSTRIES GROW, THERE IS INCREASING DEMAND FOR PEOPLE WITH STEM SKILLS.

SCHOOL: Education up to about the age of 16

THE ROUTE TO

SENIOR SCHOOL: Education from about 16 to 18

A MATHS JOB

UNIVERSITY: Studying for an undergraduate degree and a post-graduate degree, such as a master's degree and a doctorate

▼ A science qualification could take you to one of the most prestigious colleges on the planet, such as Oxford University or MIT.

SUBJECTS AND QUALIFICATIONS

For each job, we've shown what subjects you can study as you move through education from school to university and beyond, and what further training you would need. These are quite general because what you study for a particular qualification will change depending on which country you are in.

▼ Predicting powerful hurricanes requires some incredible number-crunching.

CRACKING CODES

KEEPING OUR VITAL DATA SAFE IS BECOMING A VERY IMPORTANT JOB.

Cryptology uses maths codes to make sure any information that is shared online can only be read by those who have the key to that code. This is called encryption.

The job of the cryptologist is to make sure that our information is protected from people who are trying to find our personal details to use for illegal activities. These can include identity theft, taking money from bank accounts or making telephone calls using somebody else's number. Cryptologists create codes that are meant to be impossible to break, but they are also involved in trying to crack other people's codes.

▶ The US National Security Agency (NSA) has its headquarters at Fort Meade, Maryland.

CRYPTOLOGISTS ALSO WORK FOR THE SECURITY SERVICES TRYING TO LISTEN IN TO THE MESSAGES OF CRIMINALS. TO DO THIS, IT'S ALSO HELPFUL TO SPEAK AT LEAST ONE FOREIGN LANGUAGE, AS MESSAGES COULD COME FROM ANYWHERE IN THE WORLD.

WHAT YOU DO

As a cryptologist, much of your work will be office-based. You will use your maths skills to create new codes and test those codes to make sure that they cannot be broken. You will also go back to any codes being used to make sure that they are still reliable. Because security is so important to companies and governments, you will be an important member of a team protecting all the information held.

▶ Banks use coded card readers to protect people's account details.

WHERE YOU WORK

The number of opportunities for cryptologists is growing all the time as more and more of our lives move online. You'll find work with banks, computer companies and other businesses both large and small. Many cryptologists are employed by the police, military and security services, such as GCHQ in the UK and the NSA in the US.

SCHOOL: Computer science and maths

THE ROUTE TO

SENIOR SCHOOL: Computer science and maths

CRYPTOLOGY

UNIVERSITY: Maths or computing science. Some universities offer degrees in cryptology

DURING WORLD WAR II, THE GERMANS USED A MACHINE CALLED ENIGMA THAT COULD CODE MESSAGES WITH A POSSIBLE 159 QUINTILLION (THAT'S 159 FOLLOWED BY 18 ZEROES!) COMBINATIONS.

TRANSPORT PLANNER

TOP MATHS SKILLS ARE NEEDED TO GET PEOPLE FROM A TO B AS EFFICIENTLY AS POSSIBLE.

Transport planners improve and manage road, rail and airport links. Whenever a new building project is started, then transport planners are involved right from the start. They have to make sure that the new homes, offices or shops being built are easy to reach and that they do not create any transport problems in the surrounding area. Get the design right and we'll all be able to travel quickly, safely and in a way that protects the environment.

THERE ARE MORE THAT 250 MILLION CARS AND TRUCKS IN THE UNITED STATES ALONE.

WHAT YOU DO

As a transport planner, you will spend a lot of your time examining statistics. These will help you predict what will happen when a new road, railway line or airport is built. You will be working as part of a team that might include town planners, architects and people concerned about the environment. You might also be involved in meeting members of the public and asking them what transport improvements they would like to see in their area.

WHERE YOU WORK

Most people in transport planning work for public bodies, such as city authorities and government departments that deal with transport issues. Transport planners can also work for private companies that work in transport, such as rail and bus companies. There are lots of opportunities to work internationally as well.

▼ Hong Kong International Airport is built on an artificial island, and planners had to design road and rail connections to the mainland.

◄ Transport planners need to design link roads to connect motorways to local networks.

SCHOOL: Maths and science

THE ROUTE TO

SENIOR SCHOOL: Maths, physics and geography

TRANSPORT

UNIVERSITY: Maths, physics and civil engineering

PLANNING

MANY COUNTRIES HAVE TRAFFIC PLANNING ORGANISATIONS THAT OFFER PROFESSIONAL TRAINING AND QUALIFICATIONS FOR ANYBODY WHO WANTS A CAREER IN TRANSPORT PLANNING.

MAPPING THE PLANET

CARTOGRAPHERS MAKE SENSE OF A WHOLE WORLD OF INFORMATION.

You might think that the world has been well–mapped by now. But the landscape around us is constantly changing and the need for new maps is growing all of the time. Cartographers are called upon to create all kinds of specialized maps. A cartographer has to gather this information, sometimes from satellites in orbit, and convert it into a form that is useful.

SCHOOL: Science, maths and geography

THE ROUTE TO

SENIOR SCHOOL: Maths, science, geography and computer sciences

CARTOGRAPHY

UNIVERSITY: There are some universities that offer degrees in Geographic Information Systems but a degree in maths, geography or earth sciences is also useful

ONE OF THE FASTEST GROWING AREAS OF MAP–MAKING IS CALLED GEOVISUALISTION. THIS INVOLVES THE CREATION OF INTERACTIVE AND ANIMATED MAPS THAT CAN DISPLAY VAST AMOUNTS OF INFORMATION AND CAN BE CONSTANTLY UPDATED.

WHERE YOU WORK

All sorts of businesses need people with cartographic skills. You could work for companies that specialize in oil and gas exploration. Building companies and suppliers of gas, electricity and water also have to have accurate and up-to-date maps. There are also many publishers who print maps and travel guides for the tourist and travel industry. Governments and local authorities also need cartographers to assist in the planning of new roads, homes, hospitals and schools.

IT IS ESTIMATED THAT THERE ARE MORE THAN 2,500 SATELLITES IN ORBIT AROUND EARTH.

◀ This cartographer is equipped to collect information out in the field, with a laser range finder, a GPS receiver and a rugged computer.

WHAT YOU DO

The working day of a cartographer can be divided into two main parts. The first is to collect and analyse the data that is needed to create a map. If you are working on a particular project then part of this work is to decide what information is useful and what can be ignored. Once you have gathered together all of the information you need then you will start designing the map. You will have to design the map so that it can be useful however it is seen.

▶ A cartographer sets up a GPS receiver to collect data.

FEEDING THE WORLD

BIOSTATISTICS HELP FARMERS AND FOOD COMPANIES TO FEED THE WORLD.

Biologists create a lot of data in their work. This needs to be analysed and presented so that they can understand their own work. Biostatisticians will be part of a team that will grow 'trial' crops using a new seed. They will watch the crop grow and see how it compares to other crops.

Biostatistics is also used in the field of medicine and drug research to test drugs before they are offered to doctors.

THE ROUTE TO

SCHOOL: Maths and science

SENIOR SCHOOL: Maths, biology and computer science

UNIVERSITY: There are some universities that offer degrees in biostatistics or biomathematics and a degree in maths is also a good route

BIOSTATISTICS

A FEW BIOSTATISTICIANS WORK WITH HEALTH CHARITIES, STUDYING TO SEE HOW MANY PEOPLE ARE SUFFERING FROM MALNUTRITION OR HAVE DISEASES LINKED TO A POOR DIET OR A LACK OF CLEAN WATER.

▼ Plants are studied in the laboratory as well as the field.

WHERE YOU WORK

The two main areas of work for biostatisticians are in agriculture and in medicine. There are agricultural companies that specialise in creating new kinds of seeds for farmers or manufacture fertilisers and insecticides. Medical companies produce new drugs and other treatments for people who are sick. Government bodies that create the rules that agricultural and medical companies have to follow also employ biostatisticians to examine information given to them by those companies.

13

◀ Data is collected by studying how well new crops grow.

WHAT YOU DO

As a biostatistician much of your day will be spent either in the laboratory or in the office. You will usually be working as part of a team of other scientists so some of a typical working day will be communicating with others either face–to–face or through the phone or email.

THE BIGGER PICTURE

BIG DATA ANALYSTS STUDY MASSES OF INFORMATION TO SPOT THE LATEST TRENDS.

These analysts are trying to predict what people might want in the future. For Big Data Analysts this is called 'predictive analysis'. They have to examine the data to see if they can identify any hidden trends that will continue into the future. This could include what products are selling in a shop or even how government services are being used by members of the public.

EVERY DAY, ABOUT 2.5 EXABYTES (2.5 X 10^{18}) OF DATA IS CREATED AROUND THE WORLD – ENOUGH TO FILL THE HARD DRIVES OF 2.5 MILLION DESKTOP COMPUTERS.

WHAT YOU DO

Most of your working day will be spent in the office collecting and analysing data. There are plenty of opportunities to travel to other locations so that you can collect that data. You will also have to spend some of your time presenting your analysis to the organisation you are working for. This will mean that you will have to find ways to show your findings in a way that they can understand.

THE 'INTERNET OF THINGS' SEES EVERYDAY OBJECTS FROM MACHINES IN A FACTORY OR DEVICES YOU WEAR HAVE BUILT–IN SENSORS THAT GATHER DATA. THIS INFORMATION CAN TELL PEOPLE ALL SORTS OF THINGS, FROM WHAT EXERCISE IS POPULAR TO WHETHER YOU NEED TO BUY MORE MILK.

◄ This fridge is connected to the Internet and can order more food when supplies run low.

◄ Collecting huge amounts of data requires large server farms, such as these banks of computers.

SCHOOL: Science, maths and computer science

SENIOR SCHOOL: Maths and computer science

THE ROUTE TO

UNIVERSITY: Maths, business studies, marketing or computer science

BIG DATA ANALYSIS

WHERE YOU WORK

The demand for Big Data Analysts is growing all of the time. Most Big Data Analysts work in the areas of finance, such as banks, shops and in online buying and selling. Other Big Data Analysts work for market research companies. Market research companies specialise in gathering together and analysing information for organisations that cannot do it themselves.

SPORTS STATISTICS

MATHS CAN IMPROVE AN ATHLETE'S PERFORMANCE AND TAKE THEM TO VICTORY.

DISTANCE RUN BY ATHLETES DURING ONE GAME:
BASEBALL – 0.074 KM
AMERICAN FOOTBALL – 2 KM
BASKETBALL – 4.6 KM
TENNIS – 4.8 KM
FOOTBALL – 11.2 KM

The first duty of a sports statistician is to gather information on sports performances. This is usually done while the match is actually being played, noting down how well an athlete is doing or by looking at the performance of the team as a whole.

In the run-up to a match, a statistician can also analyse information about the opposing team to look for weaknesses and where they might be dangerous.

▼ An American football team may use a statistician to spot any weaknesses in their own style of play.

▼ Sports statisticians work with individual athletes and suggest improvements in training and during a match.

WHAT YOU DO

Most sporting events happen either at weekends or in the evening, and you will be expected to be there. Of course if you love the sport that you're working in then this will be a bonus. During the rest of the week, you will spend your time analysing the information that you have gathered and then presenting that information in a way that is useful for team managers, players and television commentators.

WHERE YOU WORK

Many of the big sports teams employ their own sports statisticians. You will need to build up expertise into both the team and the sport that it plays in. There are also some businesses that specialise in providing sports statistics. Smaller teams or other sporting bodies use these specialist businesses if they do not have their own statistician. Sports statisticians also work for television companies, websites and newspapers that supply sports commentaries.

▲ TV companies use sports statistics during live broadcasts to show how athletes are performing.

THE ROUTE TO SPORTS STATISTICS

SCHOOL: Maths, sport and science

SENIOR SCHOOL: Maths, sport, science and computer science

UNIVERSITY: There are some universities that have degrees that combine maths and sport science. However, a degree in maths by itself is also acceptable

SHAPING OUR CLIMATE

MATHS CAN PREDICT THE WEATHER AND CREATE MODELS OF HOW IT WILL ACT.

People working in the field of climate modelling collect data about changes in weather patterns over a long period of time. This information includes the level of rainfall, temperatures, the amount of ice at the poles and the frequency of extreme weather events like hurricanes, floods and cyclones.

Climate modellers can then build up a mathematical picture of the today's climate and see how it has changed. Using this information, they can then predict what will happen in the future.

▼ Climate modellers try to predict how often extreme events, such as flooding, may occur.

▲ Climate modellers create maps of how conditions may change, such as this one which shows how temperatures will get warmer up to the year 2050.

WHAT YOU DO

Climate modellers usually spend most of their working hours analysing data and creating models. However, you will have to spend some of your time finding ways to present your findings that are easy to understand. There are also opportunities to visit weather stations and weather ships to help with the gathering of information on weather changes.

▲ Small stations collect information about the weather.

SCHOOL: Maths, science and geography

THE ROUTE TO

SENIOR SCHOOL: Maths, science (especially physics and chemistry) and geography

CLIMATE MODELLING

UNIVERSITY: Earth science, meteorology (the science of weather) or environmental science

WHERE YOU WORK

Most climate modellers work for universities or for national or international bodies, such as the World Meteorological Organization. There are also some businesses that specialise in providing climate models for other businesses. For example, an energy company might want information on changes in climate in a particular area before deciding to build wind turbines or solar panels.

CLIMATE MODELLING CAN BE USED BY AGRICULTURAL INDUSTRIES. DATA CAN SHOW HOW CHANGES IN CONDITIONS MIGHT AFFECT CROPS GROWN IN AREAS OR WHICH CROPS COULD BE GROWN INSTEAD.

VISUAL EFFECTS

MANY MOVIES USE MATHS POWER TO ADD DRAMA AND EXCITEMENT.

20

Visual effects (or VFX) programmers are the people who create the computerised special effects in a movie. This is often called CGI (Computer–Generated Imagery). People who work in VFX programming need strong maths skills, especially with geometry, as well as computer programming and artistic abilities.

▼ Actors are filmed against a blue screen and effects are added afterwards.

WHAT YOU DO

A VFX programmer's main task is to create and run computer programs, which are then used to create a particular special effect. This could be anything, such as a fleet of spacecraft flying across the night sky, a huge monster climbing a mountain or a lightning storm over a desert. Many of these special effects could be created without the use of computers, but they would not look realistic enough or may simply take too long to create.

SOME VFX PROGRAMMERS BECOME SPECIALISTS IN ONE PARTICULAR AREA. THERE ARE PROGRAMMERS WHOSE ONLY JOBS ARE TO CREATE REALISTIC SKY AND CLOUDS OR TO CREATE REALISTIC EXPLOSIONS.

▶ A Groom Technical Director specialises in creating realistic feathers and fur, like this.

WHERE YOU WORK

Most visual effects programmers either work for television and film–making companies or for businesses that create computer games. There are also some companies that specialise in just providing special effects for anybody who cannot create special effects themselves.

THE ROUTE TO
VISUAL EFFECTS
PROGRAMMING

SCHOOL: Maths, science, art and design

SENIOR SCHOOL: Maths, science (especially physics), art and design and computer science

UNIVERSITY: Computer–aided art and design, animation and film technology

DIGITAL FORENSICS

THE JOB OF A DIGITAL FORENSICS EXPERT IS BECOMING MORE AND MORE CENTRAL TO POLICE INVESTIGATIONS.

Police forces use forensics scientists to help solve crimes. Digital forensics experts look for evidence on any digital device, such as a computer or a mobile phone.

Many people do not realise that whenever they use a digital device like a computer or a mobile phone they are leaving a trail. If somebody makes a call on a mobile phone then this trail will include who they called, what time the call was taken, where the caller was at the time and how long the call lasted.

This evidence will still be in existence even if the caller deletes it from their phone. An expert can retrieve this data and submit it as evidence.

◄ This equipment is being used to recover data from a computer hard-drive.

WHAT YOU DO

Although you will spend time searching for evidence on digital devices you will also have to make sure that the evidence you have gathered is easy to understand and can be used in court. This will mean that there will be times when you will have to work over evenings and weekends in order to help the police. You may also have to appear in court as an expert witness and help find evidence at the scene of a crime.

ONE OF THE MOST COMPLICATED AREAS FOR DIGITAL FORENSICS EXPERTS WORK IS THE AREA OF FINANCIAL CRIME SUCH AS TAX EVASION, FORGERY OR HACKING INTO A BANK ACCOUNT.

SCHOOL: Maths, science and computer science

THE ROUTE TO

SENIOR SCHOOL: School: Maths, science and computer science

DIGITAL FORENSICS

UNIVERSITY: Computer science

▼ Digital criminals can be very good at hiding evidence, so a digital forensics expert has to be better!

WHERE YOU WORK

Most digital forensics experts work for police forces. They are brought into an investigation because of their skills in finding data on digital devices. International policing organisations, such as INTERPOL, EUROPOL and the United Nations police, also employ digital forensics experts when they are trying to solve crimes that cross national borders.

Some estimates say that cybercrime cause nearly US$500 billion of damage to the global economy every year.

****

DEALING WITH DISASTER

THIS MATHS JOB MAKES SURE THAT RESOURCES GET TO WHERE THEY ARE NEEDED.

The job of a humanitarian logistician is making sure that the right supplies get to the right place in the aftermath of a disaster.

This task starts well before disaster strikes. Humanitarian logisticians see what sort of disasters might strike a region. They also collect data such as population sizes and what hospitals are available. When a disaster does occur, they are then involved in distributing aid and helping the people recover in the short- and long-term.

▲ Aid workers hand out supplies in the aftermath of an earthquake in Ecuador.

SCHOOL: Maths, science and geography

SENIOR SCHOOL: Maths, science and geography

THE ROUTE TO AID LOGISTICS

UNIVERSITY: There are some universities that offer degrees in logistics. Studying maths, business studies or management will also be useful

WHERE YOU WORK

Most humanitarian logisticians will work for charities that deal with disaster relief. Organisations such as Oxfam, the Red Cross and the Red Crescent are all involved in preparing for disasters and then acting once disaster strikes. There will also be opportunities to work in different parts of the world.

▼ Long-term help includes repairing water supplies and drilling wells.

WHAT YOU DO

As a humanitarian logistician you will spend some of your time doing office-based work using data to plan for disasters. You will also travel to places where supplies are being stored in order to see that they are ready to use at any time. If a disaster does strike you may have to travel to the affected region to make sure that supplies are arriving safely and then being distributed in the right way.

FURTHER AND FASTER

THIS MATHS JOB PUSHES VEHICLES TO THE VERY LIMIT AND BEYOND.

An aerodynamicist studies how air flows around a car or an aircraft and how that affects its performance. They will try to find ways of making that vehicle move faster, travel further or be more economical. It's not just the shape of the vehicle that aerodynamicists have to work on. They will also be involved in the design of any electrical parts to the vehicle, the fuel system that is being used and the choice of material for building all or part of the vehicle. In all of these areas aerodynamics is important.

▼ This computer model shows how air flows over the wing of an experimental aircraft.

WHAT YOU DO

Aerodynamicists create 3-D computer models of the vehicles they are designing. They will also spend some of their time in the building of real models of vehicles that will then be tested in wind tunnels. Wind tunnels show how air flows around vehicles when they are moving. Once that part of the test is over then the vehicle will have to be tested outside of the laboratory. This means that you will spend some of your time outdoors gathering data on the tests.

THE AERODYNAMICS OF A F1 CAR GENERATE ENOUGH DOWNFORCE TO, IN THEORY, DRIVE UPSIDE DOWN AT HIGH SPEEDS.

SCHOOL: Maths, science, art and design

SENIOR SCHOOL: Maths, science (especially physics), art and design, engineering

THE ROUTE TO AERODYNAMICS

UNIVERSITY: Some universities offer degrees in aerodynamic engineering but studying engineering is also a good entry to working in aerodynamics

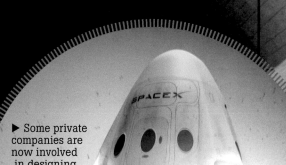

► Some private companies are now involved in designing spacecraft, such as SpaceX.

WHERE YOU WORK

Aerodynamicists work for companies that design and build vehicles, including cars, aircraft and even spacecraft. You could be working on new vehicles or improving existing vehicles. Some aerodynamicists work for government transport departments, making sure that vehicles meet any rules and regulations about safety and pollution levels.

THE NEXT BIG THING

RECORDING COMPANIES GO TO GREAT LENGTHS TO FIND THE NEXT HIT BAND.

The music industry produces a huge amount of data. This comes from music sales, both online downloads and as physical purchases, and through streaming services. Music data analysts can then use this data to see which bands are popular in which parts of the world. Record companies can then use that information to promote acts.

◀ Streaming now accounts for about 30 per cent of digital music revenues.

WHAT YOU DO

Much of your working day as a music data analyst will be gathering and analysing data from online music sites. This will also include social media websites so you can spot new bands that are just starting to build up a following. You will have to work with other people in the music industry such as marketing and promotions.

THE ILLEGAL COPYING OF MUSIC HAS BEEN A BIG PROBLEM FOR MUSICIANS AND RECORD COMPANIES. MUSIC DATA ANALYSTS CAN HELP TO SHUT DOWN ANY PIRACY SITES THEY FIND DURING THEIR RESEARCH.

▼ As an analyst, you might also have to go to live performances to monitor which bands and even which songs are becoming popular.

WHERE YOU WORK

Music data analysts usually work for record labels who sign up musicians and release their music for people to listen to. Music streaming services like Spotify or Deezer also employ music data analysts to research how people are using them.

SCHOOL: Maths, science and music

SENIOR SCHOOL: Maths, computing science and music

THE ROUTE TO

UNIVERSITY: Music, maths or computer science

MUSIC DATA ANALYSIS

GLOSSARY

AERODYNAMICS
The study of the way air moves around solid objects.

AID
Support and help that is sent to an area that has suffered a disaster. Aid can take the form of people who can supply services, such as rescue workers and doctors, or as food clothing and shelter.

BIG DATA
Huge amounts of data that is collected and stored on computers. Studying this data can reveal large-scale trends and insights into how people are behaving.

BIOSTATISTICS
Using statistics and data to study biological activity, such as how crops grow and how medicines perform.

CARTOGRAPHY
The science making maps.

CGI
Short for Computer-Generated Imagery, if refers to images and effects that are created digitally on a computer and applied to a movie or TV programme once filming has finished.

CLIMATE
The average pattern of weather in one place over a 30 year period.

CRYPTOLOGY
The study of codes and the devices used to create them.

DEGREE
The qualification given by universities after a period of study – normally for three to four years.

DOCTORATE
The qualification given by universities after a student spends several years on original research.

DOWNFORCE
A downwards force created by air passing over a vehicle. Fast cars use downforce to push them down into the road to improve their handling.

DOWNLOADS
Digital files that are copied off the Internet and onto a computer.

ENCRYPTION
Converting data into a code that cannot be read by anybody except the people with the key to the code.

EVIDENCE
Physical or verbal information that can be produced to prove a person's guilt during a criminal trial.

EXABYTE
A large unit of digital memory, equivalent to 1 million terabytes.

EXPERT WITNESS
A person who is specialised in a particular subject and gives his or her expert opinion in a court.

FORENSICS
Using scientific and mathematical techniques to help solve crimes.

GEOVISUALISATION
Turning data into maps and charts.

GPS
GPS stands for Global Positioning System. There's a network of 24 satellites that send information mapping data to GPS receivers.

HURRICANES
Huge tropical storms.

LOGISTICS
Organising and controlling the movement of things from one place to another.

MASTER'S DEGREE
A qualification given by universities. It is normally given after a degree and before a doctorate.

METEOROLOGY
The study of the weather and how it is created by events in Earth's atmosphere.

ONLINE
Something that is found on the Internet.

PIRACY
Using or taking something without the owner's permission. On the Internet, this can include posting and sharing films and music.

PROSECUTED
When someone has been charged with a criminal act and taken to court.

RANGE FINDER
A device that calculates the distance from one object to another.

SERVER FARM
A cluster of computers that is able to store vast amounts of data.

SOCIAL MEDIA
Websites and software that allow people to communicate with each other socially.

STATISTICS
A branch of mathematics that collects and examines numbers.

STREAMING
Listening to music or watching a video that is sent as a continuous stream of data across the Internet.

TRENDS
Behaviour that has become a fashion and is being carried out by increasing numbers of people.

UNDERGRADUATE
A person who is studying at a university for their first degree.

WIND TUNNEL
A building or room where wind can be produced artificially produced. Wind tunnels are used to test the aerodynamics of vehicles.

INDEX

A

aerodynamic engineering 27
aerodynamicist 26-27
agriculture 13, 19
animation 21
architect 8

B

Big Data Analyst 14-15
biologist 12-13
biomathematics 12
biostatistician 12-13

C

cartographer 10-11
cartographic careers 11
civil engineering 9
climate modeller 18-19
code breaking 4, 6
computer games 21
Computer-Generated
   Imagery (CGI) 20
computer science 15, 17,
   23
crops 12, 13, 19
cryptologist 6
cryptology 6

D, E, F

digital forensic scientist
   22 23
disaster relief 4, 24-25
disasters 24-25
earth sciences 10
encryption 6
Enigma machine 7
environmental science 19

EUROPOL 23
fertilisers 13
food production 4
forgery 23
Formula One 4

G

GCHQ (Government
   Communications
   Headquarters) 7
Geographic Information
   Systems degree 10
geovisualisation 11
GPS receiver 11
Groom Technical Director
   21

H, I, L

Hong Kong International
   Airport 9
humanitarian logistician
   24-25
hurricanes 5
identity theft 6
insecticides 13
'Internet of things' 15
INTERPOL 23
laser range finder 11

M, N

market research 15
medicine 13
meteorology 19
MIT (Massachusetts
   Institute of Technology)
   5
movies 20-21
music data analyst 28-29

music industry 28-29
NSA (National Security
   Agency) 6

O, P

Oxford University 5
police 22, 23
piracy 28
predictive analysis 14

R

record labels 29
Red Crescent 25
Red Cross 25

S, T

satellites 10, 11
server farms 15
Space X 27
sport 16-17
sports statistician 16-17
STEM (Science, technology,
   engineering, maths) 5
streaming (music) 28
transport 8-9
transport planner 8-9

U, V, W

United Nations Police 23
VFX programmer 20-21
visual effects (VFX) 20
weather 18-19
wind tunnel 26
World Meteorological
   Organisation 19